Don't Be Dramatic, Light Her Up

By Fatima Abukar

Fatima Abukar

Cover Art by Haruki
Instagram handle: haruki.design

For the eyes that saw the beauty in my flaws

For the ears that listened to me even when I did not speak

For the hands and feet that held me up in times of severe
struggle

And for the head that held the heaviest crown throughout

- *For the writer of these pages...*

And like you taught me to

let us create art from the pain...

-    *Words of empowerment from me to myself,*

and to you the reader

Contents

Fatima Abukar

The Reflection
The Reflection

Fatima Abukar

Lewis' Alice

What happened to me? What happened to the spontaneous girl who always wanted adventures? What happened to the girl who wanted to help young children struggling with their mental health like she was? What happened to the girl that would run wild in the fields even when the daffodils were burning because she'd try to save them? What happened to running away and travelling the world? What happened to never settling and going crazy? What happened to breaking the rules if it doesn't harm anyone? What happened to *me*? I was so enthusiastic, and happy, and excited, and just full of adventure. Where did the Alice in me go? Maybe the Lewis Carroll lost himself on his way and let go of the Alice on paper.

Fatima Abukar

Drop it and it's broken

It
hurts.

It still
hurts you
know - It still

does, and even
though I'm happy,

and I'm good most of
the time, I'm still sad, you

know. I'm still broken. I still
haven't healed. And I feel like

I've dropped all my happiness
into one person's hand, And if
they drop it, then they drop me

too – It means. they. drop. me.
too. It. means. they. drop. me.
too

Excerpt from "Attachment"

"You'll never understand. You won't." And she didn't. Pandora, you didn't understand how scared I was to lose you.

I didn't. Until I realised that it was me who I was scared of losing. I was scared of losing myself once I lost her.

Fatima Abukar

The birds would still fly

Screaming -
Screaming was
all
I
could
do.

Silently scream to myself
while I suffocate myself
with my pillow so
no one
would hear me cry

But it didn't matter, because
the next morning, I would feel fine-
the world would remain the same
And the birds would still fly

Reliance

Escaping myself was running to you, but once you left
there was no more running.

You left me in the dark. Alone. With myself –
You destroyed me when you left.
Left me to destroy myself.

Fatima Abukar

And in the end, it's only you who destroys yourself

It breaks my heart
seeing the girl
inside
work *so* hard,
know that she's so bright
and that there's
so much
waiting for her,
just
for her
to

tear herself back down again
and watch herself suffer
until she bleeds the
last
drops
of
what's
left.

A Letter to The Love of My Life

Oh,

But the page was empty

Fatima Abukar

But you didn't

I begged you to
stop -
   STOP
     DIGGING
the mask
   into my face,
but you didn't

But mother

But mother – this makes me happy. It's made me the happiest I've *ever* been. It's made me become a better version of myself. When was the last time that you have seen me ever so stable, this fine, this happy? Oh, so happy. Mother I understand. But Mother, it makes me feel happy.

Consequences

No one truly has the bravery to be their real selves. Not everyone is brave enough to openly share their beliefs and views without the fear of being judged. Not everyone is brave enough to do what they want, to be themselves, to be who they truly are, and maybe that's because not everyone is brave enough to face the consequences –

The very consequences that come with being our true self.

- *Everything comes with a consequence so go ahead and do it anyway. Love yourself. Be yourself.*

Millions of things

There are millions
of
things
I'd
change
about
myself
if I could,
but if I did,
then I wouldn't be me,
would I?

Blithe

It's always about if *they're happy with it,*
but have you ever thought *I'm happy with it*
and just prepared yourself for the consequences,
simply because it's what makes *you* happy?

I am

I am a woman.
I am strong.
I am fierce.
I have a voice
and I will use it!

I am the future and
one day
I will be the past,
so I refuse and I repeat
REFUSE
to leave the earth
without having made
a change.

I *will* make
a change -
a change
to the world.
I will.

Stained Notepad

Sometimes I underestimate myself
and my power to write
Sometimes I forget the power of words
Sometimes I forget how writing can
make such a huge difference

I stopped writing
for a while and
I really don't know why I did

Most days I feel like I have no one
to talk to or cry to and
tonight is one of those nights that
I realise

"*Silly me* -
My notepad is
always there for me
so I can cry and cry and cry
all my sadness out
while writing it away at the same time
and I'll never have the fear of
anyone judging me."

Identity

I don't want to lose myself,
but most days I don't know who I am

Whenever you're down

Dear you,

please don't do this to yourself
please don't.

me and you both know
that you deserve more than
to let yourself go back
to where you once were

don't break your own heart.
instead hold it
hold it

I'm begging you
not to do this to yourself
again.

don't lock yourself away
it's there for you
you *can* get help.

so, when you need help
please don't refuse it
seek it instead
don't shut yourself out
please
please don't push everyone
that comes your way away

please don't
you need it
I need it
we need them

Still hurting

It's heartbreaking to know that
everyone else thinks you've fully
recovered.

And so, you start to believe it and play
along, but really, deep down inside you
know you're still hurting

Messed with Nature

I didn't bleed.
You mistook the marks you left in the soil
for my blood.

Instead,
you blocked the routes to my path.
You messed with nature.

You shook the Earth's ground so hard,
you awakened the hungry dragon.
Oh Mr –
       Oh,
           you really shouldn't have

Fatima Abukar

To think to know

And after everything
I knew it'd be okay again.
I had hopes for what was
and what would be.

I ~~know~~ thought you ~~are~~ were
right for me and I ~~knew~~
thought that there ~~is~~ was
something there worth fighting for.

And although it resulted in pain,
and hurt, and tears,
that's fine
because I now know
~~that you're still mine~~
~~and I'm still yours~~
that losing you was one of the best
things that ever happened to me.

I belong to me

As long as you're still mine and I'm still yours,
I know everything will be alright

-   *A note to myself*

Label

You are not a writer if you do not write

~~You.~~ Me.

I didn't get over you. I just got over myself.

Fatima Abukar

Dear Me

They're not coming back and that's okay.
You just come back to me and everything will be fine.

Have Faith

All I do these days is cry, all I do is cry to you Ya Rabi.
Ya Rabi please hear me. I'm trying to reach out to you,
not because I'm in pain, not because I'm struggling but
because I now know how much I need you.
Ya Rabi,
I need you.

Sanative

I'll admit I'm
still hurting,
but -
I have to
remind myself
every.
single.
time.
*Nothing. hurts
the way
healing does.*

For you

You're not coming back,
but my heart
    won't listen.

I tell her every day to
stop.
    Stop waiting.

I tell her *every day*
'please,
    just let me go',
but she sits.
weighing down

    my entire ribcage.

convincing me
    day by day.
that she's beating
for you.
    and
      not for me.

Fatima Abukar

Candle vs Forest

Darling
when he started the forest fire,
he still continued to burn the forest and
to take your resources from beneath the ground.

He had you thinking there
was still hope and you were so consumed
by the idea of *maybe just maybe,*
that you clearly didn't love yourself
enough to notice the forest fire.

You only noticed the
candle lit scent and the
small fire that
kept you warm.

Darling,
don't you see, he's
burning you down and
you're allowing him to?

Never-ending journey

But then you cleared out the forest,
for it was toxic and full of dead trees
And you grew a garden again,
allowing
it to blossom more than ever

The garden continued to
grow and it continues,
for *loving yourself is a never
ending journey*

Fatima Abukar

I miss myself

Damn, I really missed you

HER

This person I'm becoming, I really love her

Fatima Abukar

Comparison

Yes, loving myself was probably
the hardest thing ever, because like
they say, "*comparison is the thief of joy*".

I always compared my love for you
with my love for myself.
And because it never seemed to match
up so much, I'd beat myself up for it.
Which in that case wouldn't be self-love.

Maybe I didn't love myself as much as I
thought I did.

A Letter to The Love of My Life, For Real

The love of my life,
The one whom I wake up to every
morning and lay with every night.
The one who feeds me when I'm sick,
and holds me up when I am unable to
function, both physically and mentally.
You are the most complicated,
most uncontrollable and most complex being
I have ever met.
That itself is beautiful, in-fact it's what attracts
me to you the most.
For all the times I have lost you, we found our way
back together.
And for all the times I did wrong, you forgave me.
I'm here for that. I'm here because you, *you are more
than the reflection in the mirror.*
Darling *you,*
are the love of my life and always will be.
For the very life I live, I live for you
and the very life I live, I know I must share that lifetime
with you

Fatima Abukar

X

Show them the wild forest fire,
for they only saw you as the rose
with very little thorns

Her Damn Self

She was coming back for what was hers -
Herself.

Fatima Abukar

Right Person

So, thank you for what you did -
because I fell in love all over again,
And this time, with the Right Person.
Me.

Past Self

I think about you often, I still do.
I still think about you

Elamad

She is of two elements:
ambition and adventure

Live(d)

That's what she lived for
The adventures and the risks
The very risk of getting into trouble

Fatima Abukar

A Sign

And if you don't know why you're sad,
it's a sign that you're still human

So what if I'm a Writer?

And so, what if I'm a Writer
And that's how you define me?

Paint it on my face *"that's all you are"*
Aye. I am, but that's not all I'll ever be.

For you though, I feel sorry for because
you ignore the concept of *there's more to
what the eye can see*

Give me pen and paper
and you shall see that
the power of a writer is a pain
for the eyes of those who cannot succeed

Love from

Hey,

I just wanted to say that I'm sorry.

I'm sorry that I always neglect you when I meet others.
I'm sorry that I replace you so fast.
I'm sorry that I stopped going on dates with you.
I'm sorry that I don't talk to you as much anymore.
I'm sorry that I don't praise you anymore like I used to.
I'm sorry that I don't treat you like a Queen anymore.
I'm sorry that I don't give you my time.
I'm sorry that I don't put in as much effort as I used to.

I'm coming back, I promise.
Hang in there, I will come back to you, my love.

The Fire I breathe

When I pressed the pen to paper, I felt the fire catch my skin and rise. She rose and burnt marks into my skin. It was beautiful. It was elegant, and I finally felt free.

-       The fire I breathe // The forest fire.

Fatima Abukar

Become One

You played around with fire
in the forest that we grew together
so, I decided to feed off
of the elements you used
to try to take it down
and become one

I became one with the forest fire,
and now,
I have the power
to burn the entire forest down
or simply keep it warm

Roots

I am still learning.
I am still growing.
I am still learning -
learning to love myself
and today
I love myself more than ever before,
but today
I am still learning.

The Rose that stands out so much

You plan to burn the Rose,
don't you? - the one that stands out so much,
because it bothers you.
You pour gasoline over her
petals so you can light her up
because that's how *you* lead her on.
But what you don't know is that
you're feeding her soul.
(She feeds off of the gasoline. She breathes it).
You continue pouring until she
cannot absorb anymore and sinks
instead, and *only then* you light her up.
You light the fire, and it touches her
strongest petal
And you stand there,
and watch her consume all the
colours of the flames and hear her
screams of laughter.
Not because she's crazy,
not because you're hurting her
but because *you*,
the fool,
just turned a small rose into a Forest Fire
and *you*,
the fool,
are standing
right. in the middle. of her.

Promise?

And when you're sad,
please make sure you write

Write to me

Write to the world

Write to the future

Fatima Abukar

Displace

Turn your pain into art

You first

When your all isn't enough for him, that's because your all wasn't enough for you first.

When the world puts out a fire, it's because they can't handle her. She causes so much pain and chaos, but if you sit and watch, really and truly, she's absolutely beautiful.
She brings warmth and comfort.

And when the world bombards her with elements, she screams. She roars. She grows.

You roar. You, my darling, are the roaring fire.
The one he couldn't handle, because you were too much of a woman for him.

Don't let the elements take you out. Feed off of them.
Grow, my darling. Grow.

Definitive

This is about me. It always has been.

We Know

Sometimes we know the very things we need to do to
help us heal and move forward,
but sometimes we don't want to do those very things.

Come on. Get up. Move. I need you to get up and move.
I need you to keep going. Get up and do those things.

Do them.

Su

Su -

You ever had her slither around
your neck so smoothly with one end?

Position herself so precisely around
the light with the other?

And at the same time intertwine with your
mind before any human being could?

- icide

The last thing I want on my mind.

Conditional love

You can only be loved if you follow the rules.
You can't be happy if you want to be loved.
Let love find you.

Beautiful beasts and
colourful dragons

You. Go and paint your dragon all the colours that fall
from your eyes when you cry. You. Go and eat your yellow
paint because trust me when I say Van Gogh wasn't crazy,
he was *absolutely crazy. Out of his mind, he was!* And I
love that. Who cares what people think? Don't let *anyone*
tell you not to eat your yellow paint because it's different
to theirs. Hell, if your yellow paint is *pink*, eat it. And if
anyone tries to stop you from eating your yellow paint,
you spit it back in their face because the beast inside you
is the most beautiful thing on Earth, and you must love
her enough to tell them, "Dragons exist, and I love myself
enough to ignore your ignorance."

Deleterious

Why

so serious?

You can see it *in her face.*

Deleterious with her word play
You can see it in her face. I ain't talking
deck
about the ~~stack~~^ of cards when I say bro,
she Ace. But I heard *she crazy*, so keep

your distance because it's the most
significant   parts

of
your
mind
that she will
d i s c a s e

Fatima Abukar

Criminalised victim

By the age of 13,
I was taught to believe
that if a white person was
staring at me, it's because
they're prejudiced -
ironically leaving me to feel
uncomfortable in a train full of white
people rather than them being
scared of me.

Why the saddest people are the ones who always make others happy

I think that sometimes we forget
our happiness is important too
We get so caught up in making
other people around us happy
that we lose our sense of
happiness.

We lose our sense of happiness
because we find happiness in
making other people happy,
but once that feeling goes away
we no longer feel the happiness

And that's why
*the saddest people are usually the
ones who make people the happiest.*

Burnt pages

Dear Mr,

I am not a book that you can just renew. I will not let you stamp me over and over again so that you can hold me hostage on a shelf, collecting dust.

I am not a book. I am a writer.
Oh, and if you don't mind, I have new pages to write.

<   *The door to exit the writer's room is to the left.*

P.S. You can take the old pages with you, else they'll be burned. You won't be though. You are immortal.

Rebirth

To gain the courage to leave was the hardest thing.
To mourn the loss of someone who was still alive was even harder.

Who? Who is it that you mourn over?

I've mourned for so long. I've mourned the loss of someone who was still alive. I thought that someone was you, but all along it was me.

Mine

Day
by
day,
I picked myself up.

Piece
by
piece,
to realise that the
World is mine.

And the Universe is in my mind,
So why should I feel sad?
Why?

Doublethink

I don't need you. I know I don't, but I need someone, and -

I need you.

All over again

It takes an individual to love themselves.
I am aware.

I am aware that I do not need anyone.
And as much as I'm convinced that I do not need
you in my life, if I could, I'd lose myself all over again
and I'd do it impulsively, within a heartbeat.

*- no one is worth losing yourself for, but maybe, just
maybe you are.*

Neglect

I concentrated so much on how I felt about losing you that I forgot to focus on how I felt about losing myself.

I neglected myself.

The moment you neglected me, I started drifting away from myself. I no longer knew who I was, where I stood, where I belonged and what belonged to me.

Tell me your
definition of Love

That's how you defined love.
You gave it one possible definition
and that definition,
was another
human being.

Home, you called it. *Home*.
Them. They were home.
It was like they were all you knew,
all you had ever known.
You had given them your heart
without the keyed cage
And the power to hurt you.
Yet you still trusted them not to.
Silly you.

You still gave. You still stayed. You gave everything.
You gave your all, and even that wasn't enough.

So tell me again.
Tell me again: your definition of love.

Empty bottles

After I left,
I felt like
Nothing.
I felt empty.
I felt as though
I had lost it all.
I had lost not
only you,
but I had *lost*
myself,

the ambition,
the motivation,
the wildness in me,
me. ~~It~~ She was gone.
I had lost ~~it~~ all of her.
I felt as though I was
starting a new life. It
felt like a fresh start.

Not a good one but a bad
one, and cos it hurt so much,
I was resistant to change.
I did not want it. But day
by day, I pieced myself
together and realised that
I am more than what I feel.

I learnt my self-worth
over time. I slowly started to
find myself and ~~it~~ she
slowly started ~~all~~ coming back.
She started to come back
and once she comes back and
decides to stay, I know I won't
repeat the mistake of
letting her go *ever again*.

Empire

Some days I still ask myself if I'd ever let you back in.
Some days I think, *yes, I would,* but then again
I've already started building my Empire and
you don't deserve to be a part of it.

Back where I started

I'm in a state again and everything is hurting and I...

Write the book

I was hurt.

I was lost.

She screamed
and screamed
but I couldn't hear her over the
pain.

She begged me to write her
but I could not.

Instead,
I sat in silence
while she screamed my name.

Fatima Abukar

Blue Blood Moon

Everyone is unique but do you know what you are?
You are a Blue Blood Moon. You are a once in a lifetime.
And *they* lost that.

A Writer's belief

I can't believe I thought of it as a "Forever". Did I really forget my writer self?

We're not supposed to believe in Forevers.

Darling

I wish you'd be less harsh on yourself.
These lessons have only strengthened you.
You are amazing. Darling, you are great.

P.O.V

I used to wait for someone to

"Take me somewhere new because I don't want to stay here. Let's go and runaway together. Let's go and see the World!"

Now, I hold the World in my hands and see it through the eyes of the Queen that stands before me in the mirror.

Wanderlust

I want to experience all the colours of the World;
to paint, to create, and to feel every element that it
breathes

Conflict with
the girl in the mirror

I cried. I screamed. I begged.
I begged you to let me go, to set me free
but you didn't.

Instead you stared back at me
through the glass they call a mirror.
And you did it with no emotion
whatsoever.

Conflict between
the heart and the mind

I don't know if I'm just trying to convince myself that
I'm *over it*, but some days I still find myself reopening the
wounds I had stitched up earlier. just. so. I could have a few
minutes of reminiscing pleasure.

Those few minutes only last so long,
for the pain lasts longer and the walls get harder to rebuild.

Remember

Remember who you are.
Remember that *they* fell for you.
The person they fell for, that's *you.*
Don't you see? Darling you've got it all.
That's why they loved you -
even when you couldn't love yourself.

~~Un~~wanted feelings

Just let yourself feel.
Let yourself feel all those
negative emotions
because no one else is
going to do it for you.

Treasure Hunt

I was able to find myself again.
Find myself within myself and not just you.
I was somebody before you, I was somebody
with you and most importantly,
I will be somebody without you.
And this somebody will live on
and be great again.

Fatima Abukar

Asphyxia Pill

I'd rather lose my mind screaming my words
than stay sane swallowing them

Protect

A rose isn't beautiful without its petals, but
a rose isn't safe without its thorns

Fatima Abukar

Double Entendre

Don't you see how special you are?
Darling, you have so much power
Within you and the words you write.

Do not be swallowed by all the fright,

because *you, my darling,*
have the power to take
down a fire

but *you, my darling* also have
the power to form the very
mightiest fire of them all

Wo-

A woman that loves herself is the most powerful weapon
and that's why women are seen as the inferior sex.
Simply because men know what we're capable of,
and that scares them.

Fernweh

She fell in love.

She fell in love with books,
with stories she may never hear
She fell in love with places of the unknown,
those she will never visit, smell or see
She fell in love with people,
those she will never meet and those she will never be
She fell in love with adventures she will never touch
but most importantly,
she fell in love with herself

Let

Let yourself.

Let yourself heal.

Let yourself be.

Let yourself breathe.

Let yourself free.

A letter to the reader of these pages,

Thank you for listening to me, for joining me on my journey of emotional events, for holding my words in your hands and keeping them safe with you.

Thank you for feeling every emotion with depth and complexity.

Thank you for being.

Thank you.

- Fatima

Now it's your turn ...

Fatima Abukar

Reflect

Reflect

Notes to self

Don't Be Dramatic, Light Her Up

Printed in Great Britain
by Amazon

10847647R00059